Preface

The first and important thing to say here is that I will use many company names and website addresses in this guide. All of these names and addresses are property of those parties and no copyright or infringement is intended or implied. I use those names and websites only as a reference as to what has worked for me for years.

I do not receive any money from any company or website mentioned.

Let me start by telling you that even though I am not a programmer or even a computer expert in the true sense of the term, I do have very extensive knowledge of all MS operating systems, from a "user" point of view.

However, I am one of the types of people that really like to know how "things work", so I do like to "Google" search to find out things that I don't know or understand.

I have written this guide for others, like me, who just want to know the quick and easy way to get things done. I really am not interested in "scripts" or how they work or what they do. Just give me simple programs to make my computing life easier and safer.

My first computer was a "Commodore 64" and within a few months I switched to an "IBM PC Junior". This was, by today's standards, the "model T" of computers.

Back in those days we had no internet at all. Our "back-up" or data storage was a simple cassette recorder that connected to our computer and when I wanted to "save" anything, I had to give it time to record and save the data on to a standard cassette tape (like the ones that you used years ago in your car or home audio systems). I then had to deal with the labeling and storage of all of the tapes.

My first "real" computer was a home-built that I put together with parts purchased locally, and much to my surprise, it actually worked. I loaded it with Windows NT operating system. Back then the whole system cost me a small fortune of about $3,000, and back in those days that was a lot of money.

Since that time, I have used every Windows operating system that MS has come out with. That includes NT, and every major version of Windows that has been released. There have been good ones and bad ones. There have been ones that worked flawlessly and ones that locked up for no apparent reason.

I know almost nothing about the Apple Mac operating system even though I do own a couple of iPhones and an iPad 4 and an iPad mini.

I am not even completely sure how many different computers I have owned, but it is somewhere around twelve or maybe a few more.

My personal MS Windows favorite up to now was the tried and true Windows XP Pro that I had on a total of three different computers, one desktop and two laptops.

However, since I always try to stay up to date in both hardware and software, I recently (6 months ago) purchased a new Acer Aspire V5 with a full 10 point touch screen and Windows 8.0. The very day that Windows 8.1 was released, I upgraded to that version, which I am using to write this literature.

There are the "haters" out there that always find something bad or wrong with every new version of Windows and 8.0 had more than its share, as does 8.1, but I am just being realistic when I say that 8.0 and 8.1 are both very good operating systems IF you take the time and energy to be open minded and learn the new system. I personally took about an hour to learn 8.0 and then maybe 15 to 30 minutes to learn the upgrade to 8.1 and this operating system is fast becoming my favorite of all of them. I like to learn as I go along, which I still do today.

I am constantly being asked by friends, neighbors and "friends of friends" to "fix" their slow running or non-running computers and in most cases is a laptop, and in all cases it is because the owner was not careful and/or lack any concern about normal maintenance needed. The sad part is that after I get it working back to original, I will put a "read me now" Word document on the start screen telling the owner how to maintain it in the future. This document is almost never read and if it is, the directions are never followed (because most people are too lazy). My questionable solution to this is that I have started telling people that I will repair it for free (which I have always done) the first time, but every time after that they are going to have to pay. I doubt if that will even work. It is human nature to use but not maintain a computer.

In this age of computer hacking by both the illegal hackers trying to steal money AND by almost every government around the world, it is important to do whatever is possible to protect yourself.

This is what this manual is going to try to do for you.

I will start by explaining some of the programs that you really need to add to your operating system and in all cases, they are free "shareware" programs that won't cost you anything except time to find and install them. I will then explain some programs that are installed in Windows versions and how to use them to your advantage.

If you paid to obtain this manual then I hope you are serious enough to take the time to "do things right" and take my suggestions seriously.

My personal pet-peeve is people that allow young children and even up to teen-age years to operate their computer un-supervised on the "administrator" account. Young people do not know the ramifications of having a serious computer virus or having somebody steal passwords or bank accounts.

If you see a real need to let young people use your computer, please make sure that you "log-off" of the administrator account and let them use a "limited account" in their name.

This is in the same line of thought as people that hand a smart phone to a small child to play with and then wonder why it doesn't work correctly. If they really need something to play with, buy them a cheap electronic toy and don't give a child your expensive smart phone or tablet to play with.

As for being "paranoid" as some people call it. No, I am absolutely not paranoid, but I am a realist and I do understand what both good (government) and bad (hacker thieves) people are capable of doing on computers.

Several years ago there was a movie starring Will Smith called "Enemy of the State" about all of the electronic things the government could do with computers and satellites. Back then it was considered fiction for the most part. Now there has been a renewed interest in this very movie and you can find it on almost any movie site now, because almost 100% of the things in the movie have now come true. Watch it and learn from it.

A FEW WORDS ABOUT FREE WI-FI..................................

Free Wi-Fi is so appealing to everyone and it is almost everywhere. You can find it in a Starbucks, McDonalds, almost every mall and restaurant. But along with the free cost and convenience comes the "down-side".

Hackers can sit in the same area and hijack your signal. They can route you through their Wi-Fi service while making you think that you are using the real service provided. In doing so, they can intercept your messages, your emails and most of your passwords. They can also install a virus "Trojan horse" that can infect anyone that you communicate with, and you won't even know it happened because you "didn't open any emails". No, the problem came right from that free Wi-Fi.

If you must use the internet while on-the-go, a better solution is to use a broadband card (USB) and pay a small amount for the added security. A broadband card uses the cellular system directly and still can be hacked, but it is much harder to do. Hacker thieves generally take the path that is easiest and most productive which is that local free Wi-Fi system.

There really is no such thing as being 100% safe from hackers and spying as long as we are throwing electronic signals up into the air for anyone with the proper equipment to catch. The only reasonably foolproof way to avoid this is to always use hard-wired Internet, which none of us want to do. And even that won't eliminate the possibility of Internet hackers and spies it will only eliminate the ones that rely on wireless signals.

CLOUD COMPUTING.......................................

Come on people and let's do a tiny bit of logical thinking here. Why in the world would you send all of your sensitive information into cyber-space with the very real possibility that everyone could see and read it? Would you hang all of that information outside on a tree in your yard? Of course you wouldn't, so why send it into unknown space?

There are the Cloud people that say "oh, your information is completely encrypted and is 100% safe" No, nothing is 100% safe my friends and the more of your personal information that you let leave your possession, the more there is for others to steal. It is safe and secure, if you have done everything correctly, as long as it is in your possession.

Sure, I admit that Cloud computing is easy and effortless, and in most cases you don't have to do anything. All of your data is sent to the Cloud automatically.

But, think about this, all a hacker or spy needs is that one single password for your Cloud account and he has access to everything you have and do.

Cloud storage is a misunderstood phrase for most people. What Cloud storage really is are a series of computers connected together by a single program that causes all of the connected computers to act or react as one computer. In all cases, these "Cloud computers" existing computers that have just had a cloud program added to them.

Now let's think about that for a moment. It is widely known that most well known computers have been hacked already. These include, but not limited to, the

US DOD computers, Yahoo's computers, several major credit card computers, and so on. So, you somehow think that because they "advertise" that all of your information is 100% safe, that it really is. There just is no such thing.

Try not to fall for the "easy way" of doing things. Think about the possibilities of lack or loss of security before you commit to such things.

Most people use the Cloud services because it works automatically and you don't have to spend that few minutes a day or a week to back things up. Is our time really so important that we are willing to sacrifice a few minutes for our privacy?

I am constantly sent messages trying to get me to use several Cloud services. There is one included on MS 8.0 (8.1) and one included free from Acer with this laptop. I refuse to use any of them.

Would you allow a total stranger to hold your wallet or purse? Then why would allow a stranger to hold all of your personal and sensitive information?

So now we start…………………………….

DOWNLOADING THINGS THAT YOU SHOULDN'T

I shouldn't have to tell you this, but there may be a few people out there that do not know this.

NEVER open any email attachment from anyone that you do not know. I don't care what the attachment is labeled. The hackers use an endless array of names for attachments just designed to make you open it. Things like "naked pictures of (some famous person)", "video of you drunk" or even harmless sounding names like "pictures of your family" or "I love you". If you do not know the person that sent it to you DO NOT open it.

Another reasonably new ploy is to put a virus inside of a document and then change the name and icon of that document AND THEN put it in a "zip" file. Your security system misses it because it only scanned the zip file and not the contents of the second file inside the zip file.

Just develop the habit of not opening anything that might be questionable or responding to anything that could be a scam or "phishing" attempt.

This is a good place to insert a short story that happened to me a few years ago. I received an email from my bank. It said that there was a "problem" with one of my two debit cards. It asked me to call a toll free 800 number of the "security division" of the bank to resolve this issue. So I called the number. The man on the other end answered by using the name of the bank and said he was the security division and then asked me for my debit card number..............I really didn't like that as the first question, so I said "never mind" and hung up. I got into my vehicle and drove to the nearest branch of my bank and walked in and asked to see a manager or assistant manager. An assistant manager (lady) asked me what she could help me with and I showed her the email on my iPhone and asked her if she knew what that number was. She smiled and said "yes, that is our bank security department". We both laughed and she dialed the number on her bank phone and I resolved the issue.

In that particular case, someone had somehow obtained my debit card number and had booked a 7 day cruise in the Mediterranean paying with my card. The bank's computers kicked the charge out for investigation because I had never been to Italy and there were no related charges for airfare from Texas to Italy. They have a great computer system. They told me to cut up that debit card and the next morning FedEx delivered a new card to me.

WEBSITE DANGERS………………………..

It has been widely said and known for years that porno websites have the highest number of hidden viruses and embedded tracking cookies of any type of website. What else can I say about this? Just say "no" to these sites.

The standard "joke" among computer people is that if you really need to go to a porno website, do it on a friend's computer.

First let me tell you about some really good free programs that everyone should have and be running on a constant basis.

I will list the homepage of the program "IF" there is a homepage available, however, all of these programs are also available on many download sites such as (but not limited to) CNET.com, Downloads.com, softpedia.com and many others.

Also, you can just "Google" any of the names I use and find the website or download site.

PREY DEVICE LOCATOR (TRACKER)..........................

This is a free program that is so absolutely wonderful that I am surprised that more people don't know about it and use it. You can download it in a few minutes at www.preyproject.com

This program installs on any computer and most smart phones and gives you the ability to track where your computer or smart phone is (if it is stolen), what websites the thief is going to and if you are lucky, maybe a picture of the thief using it. It has many options to use depending on your settings at the website. Some are cute but not practical as far as I am concerned.

One option is to send a loud siren-type alarm and a screen notice that says the computer is stolen. Nope, I don't like that one because the thief will just destroy the computer, because it is of no value to him and you lose everything.

Another option is to shut it off so that it cannot be used. Nope, I don't like that one because you will never find it if it is not used.

And, if your laptop is password protected, as it should be, the thief can use it, so I can't locate it.

My choice is to have a "guess account" on my laptops and tablets that does not require a password. Now the thief can use it. Then I want to see where he is, by geo-location when he is logged onto the Internet. Then, I want to see what websites he is visiting in hopes of getting his email address or user name for a website and last, I want to see his face if possible to know who the thief is that took my laptop, smart phone or tablet.

Prey is a great free program with many features and is easy to use. I have it on every device that I own.

ERASER…………………

A program called "eraser" can be downloaded at www.sourceforge.net

There is a quirk in computers that most people do not know about. If you "delete" something it really does not delete that item. Let's say you have written a document and you have given it a name to save it, OR even worse, you have a picture or video that you shouldn't have on your computer for any number of reasons. So you press the "delete" button. IT DOES NOT delete that item. All it does is delete the name or title so that it is no longer available when you search for it, but it is still there on your hard drive.

This is the reason that when you see on TV or in the news that the police have arrested a bad guy, they take all of the computers. They want the hard drives because there are programs available to "recover" anything that has been only deleted.

The absolute worst case scenario here is that you trade-in, sell, throw away or give away your old computer with that hard drive containing all of your personal information that you "thought" was deleted that CAN BE recovered. There are even hackers that will pay for people to go through trash and even public landfills looking for computers or computer hard drives.

This is where "eraser" comes in. This program was developed by/for the US DOD (Defense Department) to make sure that all data is properly removed.

What this program does is over-write every keystroke or every pixel of a picture with a series of random entries (like X's and O's) so that there is no trace of the original item. The number of over-writes will vary depending on your selection. I use a standard 32 pass.

It is maybe the simplest program to install and use. You go to the website and press the "download" button. When it says "run" or "save" just press "run" and sit back and wait. There will be other screens that will ask your permission to install it and a finish screen, just follow the simple directions.

To use it is a "no-brainer" type thing. After it is installed, when you right click on anything as you would normally do to delete an item, in the dialog box where the "delete" is shown, you will also see the word "erase". Just click on erase instead of delete. Instead of deleting the item in a fraction of a second, it may take several seconds, depending on the size of the item being erased. Videos and movies can take considerably longer, possibly several minutes.

In addition to erasing individual items, you can also right click on your "trash" or "recycle bin" and there will be an option to erase the contents of that also.

There is also another option in the program that allows you to erase all of the "unused" space on your hard drive. In other words it erases your previously "deleted" items.

This option can be found in the main program of eraser when you open it.

OLD HARD DRIVES…………………………………

If, for some reason you end up with a hard drive that does not operate (spin), then you really need to destroy it in such a manner that the disks inside are also destroyed. Smashing with a hammer enough times that you can see the interior and that the magnetic disks are broken will do the trick.

DO NOT TRACK ME PLUS……………………………

Next is a program called "Do Not Track Me Plus" by a company called Abine (www.abine.com). It is another self-running program that blocks most of the companies that are tracking your every move on the Internet (the companies claim that they track you so they can send you "targeted ads"). This program has an icon that it places in your toolbar at the top of your page that you can click to see who was trying to track you, who was blocked and who was not possible to be blocked. I just never press the icon and let the program do what it is designed to do. Again, it is simple to install just by pressing "download" and then "run" (and not "save") in the permission box and follow the directions. There is another program with the same (very similar) name, but I prefer the original program by Abine.

CCLEANER (by Piriform)……………

This is not a security tool but is a speed-up program.

When you type in a wrong Internet address this becomes a very similar mistake to the correct address and is recorded on your systems registry. Every time after that mistake, when you type in an address, your system searches all of the previous entries, as well as the mistakes, before it opens that page. Having a lot of mistakes, as we all do, will slow down the running speed of your system.

When you install this program be sure to click that you want an icon placed on your desktop.

CCleaner opens a dialog box and allows you to remove those mistakes. It is a two-step process. The dialog box that opens when you click on the CCleaner icon has four options on the left side, the top one being labeled "cleaner". This option removes all of the un-wanted and/or un-needed junk information such as unwanted cookies and temporary internet files. There are many options that can be added or removed by clicking the check box next to each item. I personally uncheck the boxes marked "history" and "recently type URL's" as keeping them does not cause a problem. You first should click "analyze" and then click "run cleaner"

The second option down on the left side is marked "registry" and this is used to remove all of those mistakes we make. Leave all of the boxes on the left checked and click on "scan for issues" and after it finishes click on "fix selected issues" which is really everything that it found. This whole process should take you only a matter of five or six minutes or so the first time and maybe two to three minutes every time after that.

I.P.LOCATOR (online)…………………

This use to be a program that you downloaded but it is now widely available on the Internet and is easy to use. In simple basic terms your I.P. address is where you are presently online. It can tell people where you are located, in what country, what city and in some cases even the name of you Internet service provider.

I.P. addresses are located in what are called the "headers" of every email and are not normally shown in the email itself. To see the I.P. of the sender you must find and click on the box for each message "show full headers" and there will be a long list of details that tell when and where the email came from and each transfer that it made on the way to you. What you are interested in knowing is the "originating I.P." which will be at the bottom of the long lists of details. That is where (and when) it was first sent. This number will be a series of one to three numbers separated by a dot, another series of numbers again separated by a dot and a third series of numbers separated by a dot and then a forth series of numbers. Copy this number and go to "Google" and type in "I.P. Locator". Although there are many sites that can do this for free, the one that I prefer is www.geobytes.com/iplocator In a second or so it will tell you where the email really came from and it is free.

A GOOD BACK-UP DEVICE………………………….

One of my previous laptops was an Acer netbook. Suddenly one day the screen stopped working. I checked and found that the ribbon wire that goes from the motherboard to the screen had cut where it went past the top hinge. The laptop was already about 4 years old and really was of no use to me and it was going to cost too much to repair. The problem was that I had a lot of personal information on the 150 GB hard drive that I did not want to get into the wrong hands. I also had some music and videos that I wanted to keep. I could not recover these things, or erase them because I had no screen to do it. I went to a local computer repair shop and purchased a hard drive case (mine was made by Samsung, but it is made by others also). The case comes with a circuit board that simply plugs in to the hard drive after you have removed it from the laptop. Removing a hard drive form a laptop is only a matter of taking out a few screws, removing a cover and the sliding the hard drive back to unplug it. You then place the hard drive and this new circuit board in the case and screw it together. It comes with a USB cable. What you end up with is a "stand-alone" USB hard drive. I went home and plugged it into my new laptop and transferred everything that I wanted. I then used the "eraser" program to clean the hard drive. I now have a really nice 150 GB hard drive for back-up of my data. The cost of the case (with circuit board and cable) was about $15.00.

Every so often, maybe once a month, I back-up all of my music, my music videos, my pictures and my documents on this spare hard drive, which I keep in a place separate from my computer. I keep that hard drive and my flash drives separated from the computer in the event of a break-in or home invasion.

HIDING IN PLAIN SIGHT ON THE INTERNET…………..

This is a subject that is dear to my heart. I just really don't like the idea of people (government agencies) spying on me for any reason. It is just a "privacy thing" to me. I haven't done anything wrong in the past and I don't plan on doing anything wrong in the future, but I just think that I should not be tracked or my personal communications open for someone to read.

So, to properly "hide" you need to think about what you say online all of the time. I will give you a very good example of saying the "wrong thing" on line later.

Now what is the best way to hide?

Generally considered to be the best is a program called "TOR" (www.torproject.org). But again, proper use means thinking carefully.

It is best to have a "flash drive" USB to install it on. I use several flash drives of various sizes. I have an 8GB flash drive that I carry on my keychain that has my music and music videos on it and enough space to download anything that I might want to when I am out and about.

I have a couple of 8GB flash drives at home that I use for file transfers back and forth to other computers and then I have a 1GB flash drive that is only for TOR.

The reason for this flash drive is so that there is no record of Tor being installed on my personal computer.

I downloaded the "Tor program" and the "Tor browser bundle" on that 1GB flash drive and when I use it, I insert the flash drive, use Tor and then remove it when I am finished.

Now let me explain in simple terms how Tor works and why it is driving the government spies crazy.

Tor is a network of computers all over the world. When you log onto the Tor browser, it sends your request for a webpage to many different computers, one at a time. Each computer encrypts the data before it sends it the next computer. That computer decrypts it, re-encrypts it and sends it to the next computer and so on. It never sends the information the same path twice. Eventually, you end up on a computer in some location (country) somewhere, and it shows you where your I.P. is being shown as. One time you may be working from New York City USA and the next time it could be Denmark or Sweden or Germany or many other countries. It doesn't matter where, as long as it is not the truth.

Now you can open any webpage just as you normally would, such as Yahoo or any other page and those pages can't track you.

This now gives you the option to have an email account that is really untraceable. You can go to Yahoo and open an email account and use a false name and related information and know that nobody will ever be able to find you.

You may ask why anyone would want to do this and there are a multitude of legitimate reasons as well as the obvious illegal reasons. I use it to send emails to friends that I have on the Internet in foreign countries such as Saudi Arabia (KSA), Afghanistan, Malaysia, Singapore and the Philippines. In all of these cases we are not plotting anything against anyone, we merely share a love for rock and roll music and Harley Davidson motorcycles. But, since I am a Catholic, some of the others are Muslim and a few are Agnostic, this is perfect reasoning for us to be spied on by an overly suspicious agency in some country. It is just the times we live in I am sorry to say.

The bottom line is that I have an email address that is the name of one of my favorite movie characters and it is non-traceable. I do not have that name or password written anywhere.

Now about changing some of your habits in order to make this work. There is a section on the TOR website about what you need to do to protect your identity while using TOR. Read it and take their advice because it works.

Using TOR is a simple but effective tool to guard EVERYTHING. But you have to do it exactly right and learn to think ahead of time.

One man (a bad guy) was recently caught even with using TOR. He made a couple of mistakes. First, he mentioned in an email to a friend some time ago about his fake name. The government went back and read all of his previous emails and found this "mistake". Second, he used an older version of TOR that had been compromised (hacked) by the government and did not go to the website for the latest version that the Feds cannot hack. Third, he repeatedly used the same public library Wi-Fi system and the Feds just sat there and waited for him to show up. He is now broke and in jail.

SELF-DESTRUCTING EMAILS………………………………………

These are exactly what the name implies. They are emails that you can send that will self-destruct or erase themselves after they have been read.

We have all sent emails to others and worried that somebody else (that you don't want to) will read them.

There is the obvious scenario of sending a message to your girlfriend that you don't want your wife to read and the opposite of a message to your girlfriend that you don't want her husband to read.

There are less sinister things like sending someone a message about your boss and you worry about someone forwarding that message to others (including the boss).

There are also many cases where it is just a privacy thing like maybe you need to send someone, like a loan officer, your social security number or maybe some financial information and you just want to make sure that the information gets deleted and not stored in someone's files or email inbox. And, of course, the business confidential emails regarding products services and pricing are a perfect use of this.

In the case of some self-destructing emails, the recipient receives a "link" to read the message and once they click on that link the message appears for reading and the link only works once. After the first time the link is used, it is invalid and the message is erased from the server that sent it.

Another type, which I prefer, is a message with a "timer" that allows the recipient a certain number of seconds, which you can set accordingly, to read the message, and then it will self destruct.

These types of messages can be found by going to "Google" and searching for "self-deleting email"

SECURITY PROGRAMS – ANTI-VIRUS.........................

I love this subject because in many ways it is so funny. First off all MS operating systems come with a "free trial version" of McAfee Anti Virus. It is speculated all over the Internet as to why this is done. Most reasons say that it is a "contractual agreement" that Microsoft has with the company that now owns McAfee Anti Virus programs. Even John McAfee himself made a joke video about how it was impossible to remove the McAfee program. The McAfee system is a good program, it is just that you have to pay to use it, after the first 90 days.

The simplest thing to do is to let the McAfee program run for the trial period and then let it expire. Then it can be removed using the MS "add or delete programs" feature.

After that you can load whatever free anti-virus program that you want on your system (but only use one).

As for me, I prefer the anti-virus program that was written by Microsoft. It is called "Security Essentials" on older operating systems and is called "Windows Defender" on Windows 7, Windows 8.0 and 8.1 and it is a free download and in most versions is already on your operating system.

This is a top of the line automatic anti-virus that is made specifically to work with Windows. Why would anyone use anything else?

Once it is downloaded (www.microsoft.com) and operational, it is basically a "forget it is there" type program. It is always running in the background (user settings) and scans in real time for any issues. It automatically updates itself with the latest virus definitions (user settings) and all you have to do is run a "full scan" whenever possible (once a month). It will notify you if anything is found by a pop-up in the lower right hand corner and clicking on the pop-up allows you to solve the issue that was found.

I once used a flash drive to have some decals made at a local mall and when I got home I plugged in the flash drive to clean it and there was instantly a pop-up saying that the flash drive had a Trojan virus. Two clicks and it was gone.

NORMAL COMPUTER MAINTENANCE…………………….

There is no substitute or quick way to do computer maintenance. If you don't do it or don't have time to do it, then all is lost.

You should set aside a certain day of the week and/or time of day to perform these simple and quick tasks. If you don't, you will pay for it in the end.

I try to do mine every Saturday, if that is not possible then the first thing on Sunday morning.

I start with "eraser" and check my trash or recycle bin and erase that if there is anything in it. I go through any downloads of music or videos or movies and erase any unwanted items.

I then go to my email folders and delete any unwanted emails and then empty the trash folder from the email program.

The next thing I do is run the CCleaner program to delete any mistakes that might be hidden there.

The next item is to check the hard drive for errors or "disk check" and this can easily be done on older operating systems by going to "system tools" and choosing "disk check" or in the new operating systems by right clicking on the hard drive (C:), choosing "properties" and choosing the "tools" tab.

After the disk check you should do the defragmentation of the hard drive. This is probably the longest thing that you have to do. Defragmentation removes all of those bits and pieces of everything that you have typed incorrectly or deleted, called "fragments". It also consolidates all of the usable information and moves this information into blocks of nice neat continuous segments. It takes old spaces and fills them with usable information and then leaves large usable blank blocks for new data. It makes everything easier for the programs to find and use on a quicker basis.

Depending on the size of your hard drive and the amount of data on it, defragmentation could take from 30 minutes to several hours to complete. I just start mine and walk away from it, checking every so often to see if it is finished.

After it is finished with the defragmentation I may or may not run "eraser" on the hard drive unused portions. This all depends on if I have anything that I consider highly confidential.

Last is the MS virus program. I open it and click on "check for updates" and then run a full scan. Again, this is time consuming and could take several hours, although normally do this once a month, letting the "quick scan" auto feature handle the normal scanning for me.

In reality, I only spend maybe a total of one hour or less on the weekly maintenance with the computer doing the long jobs without my help (un-attended).

ONE SMALL ITEM TO ADD TO YOUR COMPUTER………

There have been numerous stories on the Internet in the past months about hackers that can send you a virus and take over your webcam without you knowing it. One was about a husband and wife that had a webcam as a baby monitor and while they were sitting in the other room they heard a man's voice coming from the baby's room. They walked in and found some guy calling the baby's name over the internet. That IS a scary situation. In most cases the webcam hack is trying to catch females undressed in their bedrooms so it can be sold on the Internet.

Now, in Yahoo News just recently it was disclosed that the US government (FBI) has the ability to turn on your webcam WITHOUT the light coming on that shows the cam is being activated. It was stated that this would only be done with the "proper court order". However, if they can do it then a lot of others can do it also.

Install a simple cover over the webcam on your computer. If it is a stand-alone webcam, a simple piece of heavy cloth will do. If it a built-in webcam they you have to be more creative.

My webcam on my new Acer laptop has the camera and the light behind the glass touch screen at the top. A simple no-frills cover for that can be made with two small pieces of "Velcro" (hook and loop) fasteners stuck to the screen on the sides of the webcam and light and then the matching piece of Velcro hooked across the camera lens and light. That also acts as a nice cushion when closing the computer.

Don't for one minute ever believe that you are 100% safe on a computer. Don't ever think that it won't happen to you, because it probably will.

A long time ago, when I first started using computers, I also used that very tired phrase "my (the) computer made a mistake". No, that is not ever true. Computers are not capable of making mistakes, only the human computer users can do that.

Try not to make any bad or stupid mistakes. Try to keep your computer operating at the maximum speed and efficiency and always protect yourself and your information from others.

Have fun loading and using these new found programs.